S is for Solvang: an ABC

Jane Faulkner

ISBN: 978-1-09835-489-3

S is for Solvang:
an ABC

To John, Clay, and Joe

The little town of Solvang, California lies in the Santa Ynez Valley, about 35 miles northwest of Santa Barbara. It was founded in 1911 by three Danish immigrants who traveled to the West Coast with the intention of establishing a community that would celebrate the traditions of Danish culture, education, and religion. Jens Gregersen, Peder Hornsyld, and Benedict Nordentoft found what they were looking for in the rolling hills of the Santa Ynez Valley, and their efforts were so successful that today Solvang is known as both "Little Denmark" and "The Danish Capital of America."

A is for aebleskiver

An aebleskiver (pronounced "abel-skeever") is a round Danish pancake that looks and tastes a little bit like a donut. The word means "apple slices" in Danish because traditionally these were made by putting a small slice of apple in the center, but today they are usually covered with raspberry jam. Solvang is famous for its aebleskivers.

B is for Bethania

Bethania Lutheran Church was built in 1928 and was the first Danish-style building in Solvang. Inside there is a wooden ship hanging from the ceiling that is a replica of the type of ship that was used for hundreds of years in Denmark. The church is still in use today.

C is for Chumash

The Chumash Native Americans were the first people to live on the land where Solvang now stands. The Chumash people were skilled basket weavers, hunters, fishermen, and boat builders who lived in large, dome-shaped houses made of willow branches. There are people of Chumash descent still living in Solvang today.

D is for Denmark

The three men who founded Solvang in 1911 were from Denmark. They wanted to create a town for Danish immigrants that reminded them of their homeland and where they could practice and share Danish arts and crafts. Today the Danish flag flies throughout Solvang.

E is for Elverhoj

The word Elverhoj (pronounced "elver-hoy") means "elves' hill" and comes from a popular Danish folk play. The Elverhoj Museum of History and Art in Solvang documents the history of the town and celebrates Danish culture and the Danish-American immigrant experience.

F is for Fredensborg

Fredensborg Canyon is well known in Solvang because of the famous wooden windmill that stands at the end of the canyon road. The Wulff Windmill was built in 1922 and was designed to pump water, grind grain, and cut and polish stone. Today the windmill in Fredensborg Canyon is a California state historic landmark.

G is for Gristmill

A gristmill uses two large stones to grind grain. The gristmill in Solvang was built in 1820 on the grounds of Mission Santa Inés and was later joined by a fulling mill, which processed wool for cloth. You can still see the ruins of both of these mills a short walk from the Mission.

H is for Hans

Hans Christian Andersen was a Danish author who lived from 1805 to 1875. He is best known for his fairy tales, including *The Little Mermaid*, *The Ugly Duckling*, and *The Snow Queen*. Solvang's Hans Christian Andersen Museum is the only museum in the United States that is devoted entirely to this beloved author.

I is for Inés

Inés (pronounced "ee-nez") is the Spanish form of the name Agnes. The Mission Santa Inés was built in 1804 by the Spanish and is one of the best-preserved of California's 21 missions. The town of Solvang was built around this beautiful mission, which is still in use today as a parish church.

J is for Jonata

Solvang is built on land that was once part of a Mexican land grant called Rancho San Carlos de Jonata (pronounced "ho-nata"). The Danish American Company bought 9,000 acres of the rancho in 1911 and began developing their new town of Solvang. You can see the name Jonata in many parts of the Santa Ynez Valley.

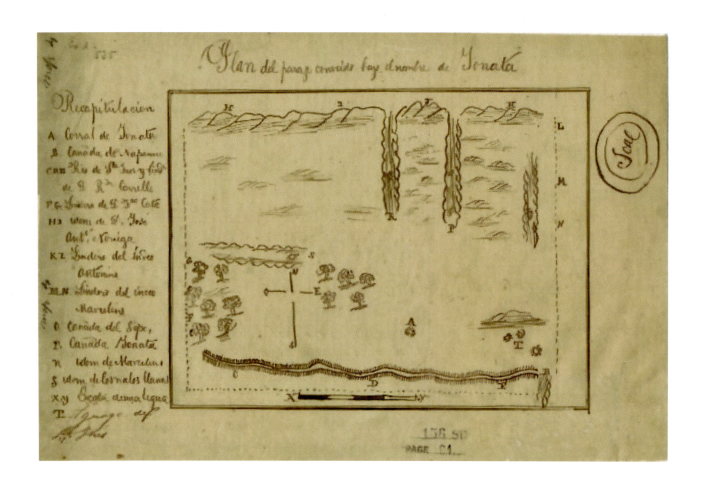

K is for Kids!

Kids have so many places to play in Solvang! Sunny Fields Park is a favorite. It has a gingerbread house, a puppet theater, a Viking ship, and a custom-built wooden playground. The park's name is an English translation of the word solvang, which means "sunny field" in Danish.

L is for Little Mermaid

Solvang's Little Mermaid sculpture is a bronze, half-size replica of the famous mermaid that sits in the harbor in Copenhagen, Denmark. The Solvang mermaid was installed in 1976 and rests on a fountain above a reflecting pool at the entrance to town.

M is for Motorcycle

The Solvang Vintage Motorcycle Museum displays dozens of vintage and rare American, European, and Japanese motorbikes. It was opened to the public in 2000 by Virgil Elings as a way to showcase his large private collection.

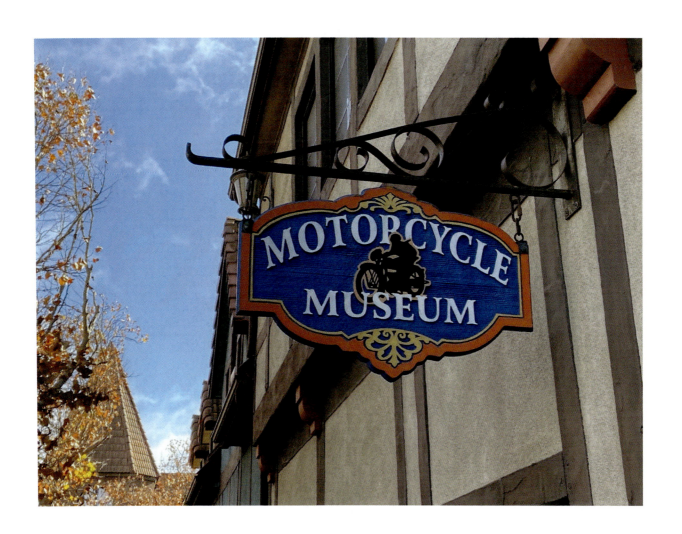

N is for Nojoqui Falls

Nojoqui Falls (pronounced "naw-hoo-ee") is a pretty waterfall that drops 80 feet over a sandstone wall and is located in one of Solvang's most popular hiking spots. The falls are a fun surprise at the end of a small canyon near Nojoqui Falls Park. Nojoqui is a Chumash word that is thought to mean "meadow."

O is for Ostrich

Ostrichland is just down the road from Solvang in the town of Buellton. It is like a farm filled with almost 100 ostriches and emus that you can feed. Ostriches are originally from Africa and emus are from Australia. They love the hot summers and mild winters in the Santa Ynez Valley.

P is for Pumpkin

All crops grow well in the Santa Ynez Valley and agriculture has always been an important part of Solvang's history. The earliest settlers were Danish farmers who chose to create a town here in part because of the rich and fertile land. In the fall you can see pumpkin patches all around Solvang, many of them open for the public to explore and enjoy.

Q is for Quail

The California Quail is a small bird that has a curving plume on its head made of six feathers. It can fly but it prefers to run. You can see flocks of quail running all over the fields around Solvang. This is the state bird of California.

R is for Rundetarn

This interesting brick tower in downtown Solvang is a 1/3 size replica of the Rundetarn in Copenhagen, Denmark, which was built in 1642 and is the oldest observatory in Europe. Solvang's tower was built in 1991 and houses a restaurant and offices. Rundetarn means "round tower" in Danish.

S is for Stork

Many of Solvang's buildings display life-sized wooden storks high on their rooftops. In Denmark it is thought that storks bring good luck, and this tradition has continued in Solvang. There are no real storks here, just these sculptures that watch over the town from high above.

T is for Theater

Theater has always been an important part of Solvang's Danish heritage, and in 1974 the community helped to build a 700-seat outdoor amphitheater in the middle of town. The Solvang Festival Theater has become a well-known landmark and a popular place to see plays, concerts, and other cultural events.

U is for Unique

Unique means one of a kind. Solvang is unique in that it is the only town in the United States that was founded by Danish immigrants who hoped to accurately re-create the Danish culture and way of life. They did this so successfully that Solvang is now known as "Little Denmark."

V is for Vineyard

A vineyard is a field of grape vines. Solvang is surrounded by hundreds of vineyards that are world famous for the wines that they produce. The grapevines grow well in the cool mornings and hot afternoons of the Santa Ynez Valley.

W is for Windmill

The seven windmills in Solvang are inspired by Danish windmills and are one of the most charming features of the town. They were built to be decorative and don't actually function as working mills, but they give the town the look and feel of a Danish village.

X is for Xmas

Solvang is known as "the most Christmassy town in the United States." Julefest (pronounced "yule fest") is the monthlong celebration of the holiday season when Solvang is decorated with lights and hosts a parade, a tree-lighting ceremony, visits from Santa and his elves, and other festive events.

Y is for Ynez

Solvang is one of five small towns in the Santa Ynez Valley, an area known for its viticulture, agriculture, and horse ranches. It is also famous for being home to Solvang, or "Little Denmark." The valley is bordered by mountain ranges and the Pacific Ocean. Ynez (pronounced "ee-nez") is a variant spelling of the name Inés.

Z is for Zaca

Zaca Peak is located a few miles east of Solvang in the San Rafael Mountains. It is not the highest peak in the mountain range but it is easy to spot from Solvang because of its rounded top. It is a very popular place for hiking and backpacking. Zaca is a Chumash word that means "quiet place."